HATFIELD

AND ITS PEOPLE

THE STORY OF A NEW TOWN, A GARDEN CITY, AN OLD VILLAGE, A HISTORIC HOUSE, THE FARMS AND THE COUNTRYSIDE IN A HERTFORDSHIRE PARISH

discovered and related by
the
HATFIELD W.E.A.

(Members of the Hatfield Local History Tutorial Class of Cambridge University Extra-Mural Board, organized by the Hatfield Branch of the Workers' Educational Association, under the tutorship of
Lionel M. Munby, M.A.)

PART 4

NEWGATE STREET
including the Manors of Ponsbourne and Tolmers

First published, June 1960
Published with index, April 2014

First published by the Hatfield Branch of the
Workers' Educational Association 1960

Published with index by Hatfield Local History Society 2014

Printed on demand via www.lulu.com

Original text by Gerald V. Millington
Line drawings by Barbara Hutton
Photographs by Henry W. Gray, Barbara Hutton and Dr. Kenneth Hutton
Index by Hazel K. Bell
Cover design by David H. Spence

This reprint was prepared by members of Hatfield Local History Society
with the kind permission of the Workers' Educational Association.

ISBN 978-0-9928415-3-9

COVER DESIGN

Top: The "Coach and Horses", Newgate Street

Bottom: Church of St Mary, Ponsbourne

FOREWORD

WHEN this series of booklets was published 50 years ago, it was rightly regarded as an exceptionally authoritative and informative work. It has since remained unchallenged as the prime source of reference for anyone interested in the history of Hatfield. Recognising its enduring value, members of Hatfield Local History Society have undertaken this reissue.

Since the booklets first appeared, some of the information contained in them has inevitably become out of date. Hatfield has been affected by sweeping changes, not least by the departure of the aircraft industry and the establishment in its place of a flourishing university and business park. Nevertheless, the original series has stood the test of time remarkably well. We know from our own research experience that it remains immensely useful and we have decided against attempting any piecemeal revision. Instead we have thought it better to reproduce the original booklets without making any changes, except for correcting obviously unintended typographical errors. An important difference is that much more comprehensive indexes have been added.

We hope that the reappearance of the work will stimulate others to undertake new research into Hatfield's more recent past.

Amongst the team who have undertaken the reissue is Henry W. Gray, M.V.O., one of the authors who took part in the W.E.A. class, led by the late Lionel Munby, which produced the original series. The others are Christine Martindale and Jane Teather, Chairman and Publications Officer respectively of Hatfield Local History Society, Hazel K. Bell, who created the new comprehensive indexes, Robin Harcourt Williams, formerly Librarian and Archivist to the Marquess of Salisbury, and G. Philip Marris who led the project.

Thanks are due to Mill Green Museum for allowing some of the original photographs to be re-scanned.

The *Workers' Educational Association,* founded in 1903, is a charity and the UK's largest voluntary sector provider of adult education, delivering 9,500 part-time courses for over 74,000 people each year in England and Scotland.

Hatfield Local History Society is an association of people interested in the history of Hatfield. The Society's aims and objectives are to encourage and undertake research into Hatfield's history, to produce publications and to provide a forum for the exchange of information on the history of the Hatfield area.

The Society is grateful to the copyright owners, the Hatfield Branch of the Workers' Educational Association, for permission to reissue the *Hatfield and its People* series. The complete list of titles is as follows:

Part 1	A Thousand Years of History
Part 2	The Story of Roe Green and South Hatfield
Part 3	Pubs and Publicans
Part 4	Newgate Street
Part 5	Roads and Railways
Part 6	Law and Disorder
Part 7	Churches
Part 8	Schools
Part 9	Farming Yesterday and Today
Part 10	Houses
Part 11A	Families and Trades (Part A)
Part 11B	Families and Trades (Part B)
Part 12	The Twentieth Century.

Please contact Hatfield Local History Society for further information about this publication.

INTRODUCTION

NEWGATE STREET seems remote and insignificant against the panorama of English history; its local history, one might imagine, would be parochial in the extreme; yet we shall meet in these pages some great names, for this small part of Hatfield parish was owned by a succession of vivid personalities, and many of them lived here; still more visited their property. "Though the historian is compelled by the nature of his work to emphasise the changing aspects in the life of a people, he fails in his task if he does not also call attention to the permanent foundation which underlies these superficial changes" (Halevy). The estate owner has been the dominant factor in Newgate Street's history for six hundred years. So this brief history is largely the story of the men and women who have owned or tenanted the estates of Ponsbourne and Tolmers.

I first conceived the idea of writing the story of Newgate Street, when, in 1956, preparing a talk, I found that there were such large gaps in the known history of the village. After enrolling in the Hatfield Branch of the Workers' Educational Association, as a corresponding member, I obtained access to a wide range of documents and other material; a more complete history of Newgate Street was revealed. In this connection I am especially indebted to the County Archivist, Col. W. le Hardy, who allowed me six months unhindered access to a manuscript held in the County Record Office. This manuscript was compiled for James Carlile by W. F. Noble in 1879. The volume contains extracts from every document, known at that time, connected with Ponsbourne, Tolmers and Bedwell Louthes.

In addition to this work, the principal sources of information have been the five standard County Histories, by Chauncy, Salmon, Clutterbuck, Cussans and the Victoria County History, also Archaeological Studies on Ponsbourne by Carlile, the County Session Books, Hatfield by Antrobus, and the following documents: Cotton Tib.B.2—1220; Cotton Claud CXI circa 1251; Terrier of Hatfield 7 Hen. IV, Rental of John Say Kt. 7 Edw. IV and sundry Inquisitiones Post Mortem.

I am also most grateful for the help given by countless private individuals: Mr. W. Branch Johnson, Mr. E. W. Seaton of Cannon Brewery Co. Ltd., the late Miss O. Bettesworth, Mrs. E. Monk, Mrs. M, Sequeira, Mr. G. Hart, Rev. E. J. Maddock, Mr. J. Collinson, Mr. Lionel Munby, and members of the Hatfield Branch of the W.E.A., to name but a few. The map was drawn by Mrs. Hutton and the photographs taken by Mr. H. Gray and Dr. Hutton.

It must be emphasised that to obtain a broader picture of the relationship of Newgate Street to the rest of the Hatfield Manor, this volume should be read in conjunction with the other books in the series. Hornbeamgate Manor played a very large part in shaping the hamlet in the early days and it is hoped that the story of this manor will appear in a later volume.

This work is in no way intended to be a complete and exhaustive history of the village. In fact, a great deal is still unrecorded, especially of the last century and a half. Many important facts are held in the memories of the inhabitants and former villagers. This source of information remains virtually untouched and I am anxious to tap it. I should, therefore, be grateful for notice of any inaccuracies and for information of events omitted from this brief history.

G.V.M.

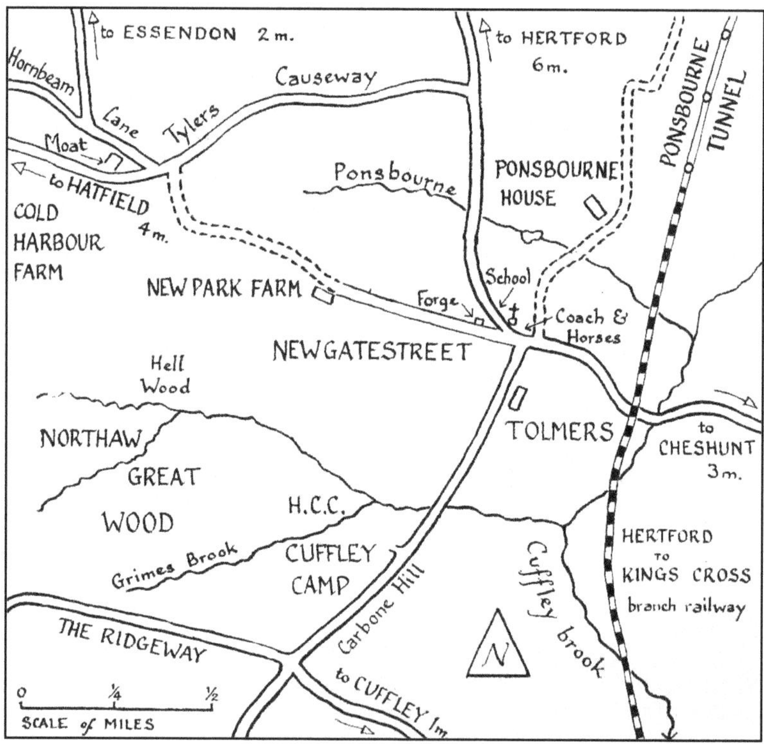

Fig. 1. Newgate Street

Newgate Street

FIVE miles south east of old Hatfield lies the village of Newgate Street, still part of Hatfield Parish and linked to it by history though not by bus services (see Book 1, fig. 10, p. 15). School-children from all parts of Hertfordshire have looked from the County Camp on Carbone Hill, Cuffley (fig. 1) northward to the church spire (front cover) less than a mile away on the next hill top and some know the village far better than many adults. Let us follow them on a tour of exploration.

Down the Cuffley-Hertford road we go, crossing Grimes Brook at almost the 200 foot contour as we enter Hatfield parish, and then climb 150 feet up to the top of the ridge. Just before the village itself, we notice a fine white fronted house on our right amongst the trees, this is TOLMERS, now an old people's hospital, but with a history dating back 700 years to when Walter Tolymer cleared the original forest to make a farm (Fig. 8, p. 20).

The playground on our left is worth a careful look from the corner by the signpost; the rough ground on the right (north) is at a lower level, and even the hedge at the far side suddenly dips down too. A change like this is suggestive; in fact the hedge here crosses the line of a Roman road, which has been traced by Mr. R. H. Reid; it runs east from Coleman Green through the middle of Hatfield and along Green Street on its way to Cheshunt (see Book 1, p. 25).

Turning left (west) at the crossroads, we soon find on our right, under a horse-chestnut tree, a blacksmith's forge with a litter of horse-shoes, showing that we are really in the heart of the country. The road continues up to Newpark Farm; it was new made soon after the Cecils came to Hatfield in 1607. Outside the left-hand gate-post is a fine puddingstone, looking rather like a lump of concrete; in fact, it is a naturally occurring rock, and there are many smaller pieces scattered over the nearby fields. This is on the line of a pre-historic trackway, marked by puddingstones at intervals of a mile or so, and traced by Dr. Rudge, going east from the Berkshire and Wiltshire downs (Stone-henge), to Grimes Graves in Norfolk where stone-age men had a mine for the flints which they used to make tools. These men probably camped in Northaw Great Wood where they fashioned their beautiful stone tools from flint. We have found the pieces they chipped off in making axes, arrow-heads and blades by Grimes Brook.

If we go back to the centre of the village and turn left (north), we notice on our right the little school next to the church, the Crown Inn, and then through a gap between the houses a fine large house on top of the next hill; this is PONSBOURNE HOUSE, now a Roman Catholic Boarding School. Turning left off the Hertford Road, we climb up Tylers Causeway, no doubt named after someone who baked the local clay into tiles, as well as pottery or bricks (Book 1, p. 19).

If we are not too "parochially-minded", we should cross over the parish boundary and look at the Moat next to Hornbeam Lane (see Book 2, p. 8). The ground here is at a height of over 400 feet and is marked by an Ordnance Survey triangulation pillar. The ridge between here and Brookmans Park radio station is the highest part of the parish; not surprisingly the farm on the ridge is called Coldharbour!

The road to the east from Newgate Street leads steeply down hill to the Hertford branch railway. This was the last important line to be constructed in Britain, and was first used in the first world war in 1918 when a collision blocked the main-line (see Book 5). Diesel trains disappear into the mouth of Ponsbourne tunnel (2680 yards long) which is the longest on the old L.N.E.R. system and has as many as five air-shafts visible in the hill above it. The huge concrete cubes by the railway bridge are anti-tank barriers which were made to stop a German invasion in 1940; as they have survived for twenty years, perhaps they will remain as visible history as long as the Roman road or the pudding-stones, which can still be seen 2000 or 4000 years later.

This southern peninsula of Hatfield parish, which we have been describing, may seem a very ordinary, quiet backwater, but along the tracks and roads which pass by it people have been travelling for thousands of years. For a long time, however, Newgate Street remained forest land, until men first began to clear the forest and settle here some 750 years ago. Before this time the Lord Bishop of Ely and his friends may have hunted the forest and some of Hatfield's many swine may have rooted for a rough existence. But only charcoal burners' huts and rough shelters for swineherds could have been found here, nothing of which there is archaeological or documentary evidence. In our own day the Enfield Chace Foxhounds meet at least twice a year outside the Coach and Horses to hunt in Ponsbourne Park.

In 1221 Lawrence de Thebrege of Waterend, Sandridge held twenty acres "next Newgate" and Walter de Godarvill one and a half virgates (perhaps 60 acres) in what seems to have been this district. The *Newgate* was not necessarily new in 1221; it marked the eastern extremity of Hatfield Great Wood and stood astride the Roman road, probably on the high ground at what is now the junction of New Park Road and the Hertford Road. The first mention of an actual gate was in 1534, when a house at Newgate Street was bought and turned into one of the lodges for the Great Park. *Street* was the English for a metalled, that was usually a Roman, road.

We learn from another survey, that by 1251 the amount of land cleared from the forest for farming had increased. The (Abbots and) Bishops of Ely, like other Hertfordshire church landlords, sought to raise the value of their property by granting out waste and woodland on its edges as assarts on a free tenure, that is the tenant paid a money rent instead of having to work for the lord as a villein or serf. This gave the tenant an incentive to clear and cultivate previously uncultivated land. The village of Newgatestreet was born out of such *assarts*. It probably never had great unhedged, *open fields*, like those of central Hatfield in the middle ages, divided into a chequer board of allotment-like strips.

By 1251 Richard de Blancheville held the largest holding; Robert Forestar was clearly a leading personality; he was a member of the twenty-six man Hatfield jury responsible for the survey. Walter de Tolymer held thirty acres of newly cleared land. William Suffel held half an acre at Newgate Street. This may have been for a farmstead devoted to stock breeding, making use of grazing rights in the forest; for Suffel was a butcher with a stall in Hatfield market, for which he paid "18d. on the feast of St. John the Baptist".

These small assarts around the Newgate coalesced into two estates, which acquired manorial status—Gacelyns later absorbed into Ponsbourne, and Tolmers. Tylers Causeway developed differently. The first tenements on the Causeway seem to have been cleared of trees about 1370; Thomas Tyler, who may have given his name to the causeway, was holding land here in 1377. Thirteen acres were under development as small holdings by 1406, but none of them was absorbed into the two large estates.

FREE TENANCIES	
Richard de Blauncheville	66 acres worth 15/5d.
Robert Forestar (of Ponsbourne)	23 acres 1 rood worth 7/9d.
Walter Tolymer	30 acres worth 10/-
William le Paum	1 acre worth 4d.
William Suffel	½ acre worth 2d., and a butcher's stall worth 18d. in Hatfield Market.
	Total: 120 ½ acres

Fig. 2. Holders of land at Newgate Street in 1251.

Ponsbourne and Gacelyns

PONSBOURNE, or rather Pumelesburne—there are innumerable spellings—is first mentioned in a legal deed of 1229. It is the stream which is referred to; the Ponsbourne drains Tylers Causeway, falls sharply before entering the park to which it has given a name, and joins the Cuffley Brook near the railway line. An old English personal name, Pumel or Pumi, is the probable origin of the first part of this name, "burna", meaning a stream, of the latter part. In 1251 Robert Forester paid 7s. 9d. for twenty three and a quarter acres in Newgate Street. Documents of 1292/3 show William son of Robert de Forester as holding forty acres of arable, two of meadow, three of woodland and other property. He is also described as William de Pomelsbourne; the family name had changed with the acquisition of their new property (see Book 1, p. 22). A John de Ponsbourne is mentioned in 1293 and Robert the son of William de Ponsbourne in 1308. Members of the family appear regularly as jurors and witnesses to documents. There is a mention of the heir of Robert de Ponsbourne in 1346; in a terrier, or inventory, of the lands of the Bishop of Ely in 1406 the original family holding of twenty three and a quarter acres in Newgate Street is once again mentioned.

After 1406 the family of de Ponsbourne disappears from the records, but for eleven years, from 1326/7, ten acres of Robert de Ponsbourne's land was held by GACELYNS manor; it is possible that the de Ponsbourne holding was absorbed into Gacelyns. Certainly by the middle fifteenth century the holdings were united in the possession of the Fortescues.

In 1255 Geoffrey Gacelin held land in Hatfield; in 1268 he conveyed one messuage and two carucates of land (perhaps 250 acres) to William de Valence, Earl of Pembroke. Gacelyns manor was recognised as such by 1327; it then consisted of 77½ acres of land held of the Bishop of Ely. The size of the estate was to shrink and to expand many times. Like Tolmers, it passed through the hands of many interesting and important people, some of whom lived here and more of whom visited their property. So Newgate Street, at first sight very ordinary and rather out of the way, is associated as we shall see with much of English history.

William de Valence, half-brother of King Henry III through his mother Isabel, the wife of King John, came to England in 1247, at the instigation of his royal relative. He was granted Hertford Castle and firmly established himself in the district, acquiring land at Bayford. The high-handed and lawless behaviour of the nobility of the period is brought out by an incident which occurred in 1252. De Valence was accused of hunting on the lands of the Bishop of Ely, near the Bishop's palace, and afterwards of ransacking the wine cellars. The conviction of the baronage that they were above the law was an element in the baronial disputes of Henry III's reign. William was deeply involved in these and forced to flee the kingdom in 1258. He was killed in France in 1296. He was succeeded by his third son Aymer, "a tall man and pale of countenance". Aymer fought ably in the Scottish wars under Edward I and was Governor of Scotland before Bannockburn. In 1317 he was captured in France and held to ransom for 20,000 pounds worth of silver; in 1324 he was murdered while serving Queen Isabella in France. He had owned estates in twenty-five English counties with his principal seat at Bampton, Oxford. The earldom became extinct.

From Aymer's *inquisitio post mortem*, we learn that he held, in free socage, one hundred and four acres of arable and sixty acres of woodland at Gacelyns. He paid suit of court and 9s. 2d. to the Bishop of Ely for part of this property. Another part of his estate was held of Bayford manor. The woodland contained no underwood, which implies that it was well maintained by foresters and used for hunting coneys (rabbits) and deer. The arable land was "poor, worth 20/8 per annum. Price of an acre being 2d. and not more because the land is hilly and stony". The free tenants were paying 27/5 per annum rent and 15/- rent was being paid annually to the free chapel of Symondshyde. From later inquisitions it is seen that this item relates to land held in Symondshyde Manor.

The estate had thus grown to considerable proportions, and was situated partly in Bayford, while stretching into the Ely lands and containing the New Park and Tylers Causeway areas of Newgate Street. Aymer had been granted free warren in 1309 and four years later was complaining of trespass of it, but it is probable that he only saw the manor on fleeting visits if at all.

Aymer was succeeded by his niece Joan, wife of David Strathbogie the eleventh Earl of Atholl. A descendant of King Donal Bane, he was High Constable of Scotland and was summoned to the English Parliament of 1322. Dying in 1326, he was succeeded by his son David, the twelfth Earl, who although only a minor was granted livery by Edward III and paid homage before coming of age. This meant that the estates did not revert to the crown during his minority and the family were saved the considerable depredations which this would have meant. David was summoned to Parliament in 1334 and 1336. But in 1336 he went to France and was killed at an early stage of the Hundred Years War, in his twenty-eighth year. Owing to this premature death, his son was only three years old when he inherited the vast estates and they were held by the crown for the next eighteen years. The rent received by the king from Gacelyns, he granted first to Adam de Walton, then to the twelfth Earl's widow, in dower. She exchanged this rent with the king, for lands in Northumberland, about 1337. David the thirteenth Earl died in 1375.

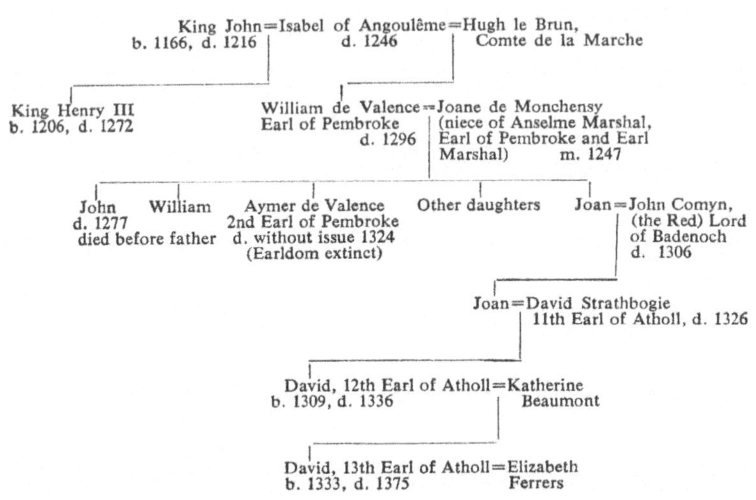

Fig. 3 de Valence-Strathbogie families.

The de Valences and Strathbogies could have had little or no interest in Gacelyns apart from its income and hunting value. It is therefore doubtful if any large house was built on the manor. There may have been a hunting lodge and a demesne farmstead.

The rent, which the king received from Gacelyns, was £6, paid in 1335/6 by Ralph de Blithe a London innkeeper. What happened to the manor between this date and its purchase by Sir John Fortescue in 1447 is far from clear. There seem to have been at least seven tenants or holders of the manor. No doubt the Crown did its best to milk the estate during the thirteenth Earl of Atholl's long minority. The period was one of economic decline; all over England marginal land ceased to be cultivated; some of the arable and pasture of Gacelyns may have reverted to scrub.

Gacelyns Manor disappeared as such when Sir John Fortescue fused it with other land in the neighbourhood to create the new manor of PONSBOURNE. Since the time of the Fortescues, Ponsbourne has always been the largest estate in Newgate Street, as it still is. Twenty-two acres of Ponsbourne land had been rented by the owner of Gacelyns for 3s. 4d. in 1326; the Strathbogies were paying only 3d. for ten acres of this land in 1336; the whole twenty-two acres still belonged to the de Ponsbournes in 1406, but by the middle of the fifteenth century it was Sir John Fortescue's. He probably called his new estate from this property, rather than Gacelyns, because the manor house which he built was sited on the old de Ponsbourne lands. The building was built of brick in the shape of a letter "E". The Fortescues held Ponsbourne in Knights Fee of the Bishops of Ely and of the Duchy of Lancaster.

Sir John Fortescue's new estate was built up by the consolidation of properties in several parishes and manors. He began, in 1439, by purchasing Bayford Manor and this was followed, in 1447, by "the Manor of Gastlynniggys" and six messuages and two hundred and fifty acres in Hatfield, Essendon and Little Berkhamsted. Finally in 1449, thirteen messuages and three hundred and eight acres were purchased in Berkhamsted. In addition, Sir John purchased Mimms Hall manor and Winderich manor in St. Albans.

Sir John Fortescue was descended from an illustrious Norman family, the members of which distinguished themselves in soldiering. But the family had turned to the legal profession and Sir John's uncle, another Sir John, was Lord Chief Justice in 1442. Sir John himself had been knighted by Henry VI for his part in the War of the Roses.

Sir John was succeeded by his son John who also supported the Lancastrian faction in the Wars. He was knighted and created Porter of Calais by Henry VII. On two occasions he was elected Sheriff of the County of Hertfordshire.

At the second Sir John Fortescue's death in 1500, the vast estates passed to his second son, another John. He seems to have suffered somewhat from the expensive living of his predecessors, but his sale of Mimms Hall Manor to John More (father of Sir Thomas, see book 2,

p. 9), in 1510, seems to have put him back on his feet. However, he died at an early age, in 1518, and was succeeded by his infant son of two years, Henry Fortescue. The estates were administered by Henry's mother and step-father, Francis Bryan, during his minority; they continued to live at Ponsbourne after Henry reached his majority. He leased the property for eighty years to Sir William Cavendish and in 1538 sold the reversion of the manor together with Winderich to Sir Thomas Seymour.

Ponsbourne was still held in knights fee of Hatfield Manor and in 1538, HATFIELD passed to the crown, the Palace becoming a Royal Nursery. Seymour married Catherine Parr, Henry VIII's widow and eventually took up residence at Ponsbourne in 1547. It did not take him long to become acquainted with the Princess Elizabeth at Hatfield and he was soon endeavouring to persuade the future queen to succumb to his charms. On Catherine's death, Seymour formed the project of marrying Elizabeth, but his plans misfired; he was executed in 1549. Ponsbourne reverted to Henry Fortescue, who conveyed it to the crown "for divers good causes and considerations".

In 1553 Sir John Cocke of Broxbourne bought Ponsbourne, together with Templewicombe, for £1,108 15s. In the same year Sir William Cavendish took up his unexpired lease; the terms of this lease state that the forty-three acres of woodland, valued at £20 a year, were reserved to the crown. Six of these forty-three acres were of oak and beech of a hundred years growth and these six acres were valued at £10 5s., over half the total! Cocke had bought the manor as an investment and he continued to live at Broxbourne after his purchase. There is no evidence that the Cocke family ever lived at Ponsbourne; in 1598 William Graye was holding the lease. The manor retained a high value throughout the first fifty years of the Cocke ownership; an assessment of 1576 was for the high figure of 72s.

Sir John Cocke died in 1556 and was succeeded by his nineteen years old son, Henry, who became Sheriff of his county in 1574. Sir John Neale in his *The Elizabethan House of Commons* has some interesting comments to make on Henry Cocke, who was knighted in 1590. In 1584 Henry Cocke precipitated the first recorded disputed parliamentary election in the county: "an ambitious gentleman, who had already sat in two parliaments, for different boroughs—(he) evidently thought that the time had arrived to strike for the crowning glory of becoming knight of the shire. He wrote to Charles Moryson—'I know my own private credit is not such in the shire (although I account myself very much beholding unto my countrymen) as of myself I can clearly carry away so great a matter as that is'. He asked Moryson out of friendship to support him". Moryson was already pledged to the other candidate. Cocke won the election. "The rift thus created or widened in the county seems to have continued for many years, and we catch occasional glimpses of it. In 1586 Henry Cocke was again returned to parliament,—Then in 1593 we hear of another contested election, when Edward—now Sir Edward—Denny once more challenged Cocke and again was beaten". In 1601 Cocke was made Cofferer of the Queen's Household. He died in 1609 possessed of the manors of Broxbourne, Cheshunt, Anstey-ad-Castrum and Ponsbourne. Winderich had been sold to Sir Nicholas Bacon (father of Sir Francis) in 1574; a small farm in Bayford, part of Broxbourne, had also been sold. Maybe these sales were the first signs of the financial difficulties that the family ran into during the next thirty years. Sir Henry's widow, Ursula, continued in possession and in 1614 was mortgaging Ponsbourne to Arthur Turner of the Middle Temple, but her son-in-law Sir Edmund Lucy managed to recover it in the same year. By 1620 the Lucys really were in trouble and Henry, Sir Edmund's son, managed to mortgage Ponsbourne to Robert Tokeley, mariner, for £600, agreeing to pay back £780 in five instalments of £30 each with a final payment of £630. If he defaulted, Tokeley became the fee simple holder. It appears that this mortgage was redeemed by Edward Sheldon from Tokeley and all parties agreed to sell the manor on Sir Edmund's death. This occurred in 1631 and Ponsbourne was sold to Sir John Ferrers a son-in-law of Sir Edmund, for £4,750.

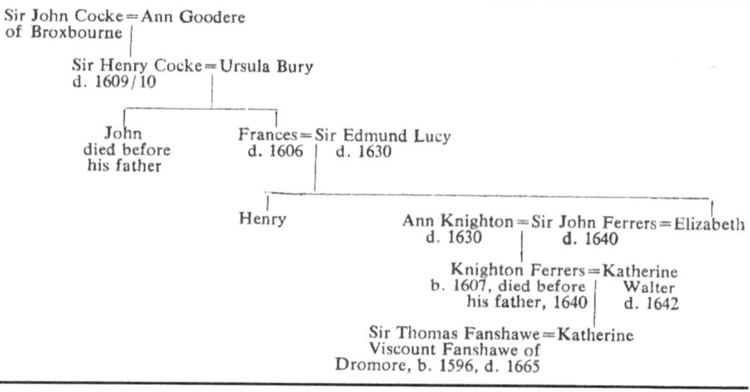

Fig. 4. Cocke family

Sir John Ferrers died in 1640 and Ponsbourne eventually descended to his grand-daughter, Katherine, and her husband Sir Thomas Fanshawe. The Fanshawes' home was at Ware; the family had made a fortune as loyal and efficient civil servants in Queen Elizabeth I's Exchequer. They lost much of it during the Civil War, for they were devoted Royalists, and raised large sums for Charles I and then had to pay heavy fines to the victorious Parliament. The Restoration brought the empty reward of an Irish Viscountcy. But Sir Thomas had had to sell Ponsbourne in 1653; in 1668 his son, another Thomas, had to sell the family home at Ware.

Ponsbourne was sold for £5000 to Stephen Ewer of Watford. Ewer was a Puritan attorney, who had already bought much land in Hertfordshire before the purchase of Ponsbourne. Like others he was able to buy land at a low price as an investment because the combination of governmental sales of Crown and Church property and sales by indebted Royalists produced a glut on the land market. The price paid for Ponsbourne covered land in Cheshunt, Broxbourne and Wormley, as well as in Hatfield, Berkhamstead, Bayford and Essendon, in which parishes the Ponsbourne estate then lay. That Ewer's purchases were to enlarge his capital rather than to obtain an estate is clear from his sales of the outlying portions of Ponsbourne within a few years. The sales brought in well over £1000, but unfortunately the changes in acreages in this period are not clearly indicated in the documents. When the manor itself was eventually sold in trust for Richard Woolaston in 1674, its acreage was about 450, something like its present day size. Ewer received about £5,500 for these acres. We have a good indication of Ewer's Puritanism at the time of the Restoration of Charles II in 1660. When the Fortescues lived at Ponsbourne they had endowed a chantry chapel in the Ponsbourne Aisle in Hatfield Church; the successive owners of the manor were responsible for the chapel. In 1660 Ewer was in trouble for refusing to pay towards repairs to this chapel and the rest of the church. This was as likely to have been a religious protest as a piece of miserliness. In 1672 Ewer obtained a license to hold Presbyterian services.

The estate which passed from Ewer to Woolaston was almost certainly prosperous and well farmed. But the latter did not hold the manor for long and Paris Slaughter purchased it for £6,000 in 1684. He owned much land in England and Ponsbourne benefitted by his ownership. But his son, Paris, who succeeded him in 1693 soon ran into financial difficulties and was obliged to mortgage Ponsbourne to Joseph Brookbank for £2,120. The manor eventually passed to Mary Clarke, sister of Paris, whose husband died in 1714 and left her with ten children. It appears that the manor house was "very stately and large" at this time; it "will cost a considerable sum annually to keep in repaire and will yield little profit to her and her children". The house had an annual value of £192 and the crop on the ground was worth £50 per annum. The house appears to have been well furnished and to have contained a few valuable paintings. In her poverty Mrs. Clarke petitioned in Chancery in 1718, to break an entail, and as a result the manor was sold to Samuel Strode, Barber Surgeon of London, for £4,148; this money was invested in the new lottery annuities for the benefit of the Clarke children. Strode also paid off Brookbank's mortgage, to the tune of £2,187; so the estate cost him £6,335.

Strode, whose son married a daughter of the fifth Earl of Salisbury, purchased another 198 acres. The acreage had doubled since 1674. Although Mrs. Clarke had a difficult time during her tenure, the productivity of the sub-manor had increased enormously since the Cockes took possession in 1553. There was no lack of buyers when the estate came on the market and the purchase price had jumped from about £800 in 1553 to £6,300 in 1718. It is difficult to give any exact idea of what happened to the value of the pound in this century and a half, but very roughly it fell somewhere between half and a third, while the purchase price of the estate jumped by eight times; the fall took place before 1660, after that date there was, if anything, a rise in the value of money. This increase in the real capital value of the estate was connected with improved farming and improved estate management. Before Ewer's tenure, the estate seems to have consisted of one large farm working most of the land and a smaller tenanted one; but Ewer divided the major portion of the estate into three farms under a bailiff and one farm and two crofts which were let to tenants. Two further tenanted crofts had been added by 1718.

Descendants of the Strode family held the manor from 1718 to 1761, when it was sold to Lawrence Sullivan for £13,590. He pulled down the manor house, as it was decaying rapidly, and erected a second mansion on higher ground above the brook. Ponsbourne had now become a desirable residence for London business men and in 1811 another member of this class, William Busk, M.P., purchased the manor. He was an inventor of some ability, improving the process for making porcelain pipes and also improving the propelling of ships. He sold Ponsbourne to his brother Jacob Hans Busk in 1819, who sold it to Wynn Ellis in 1836.

Ellis, who had amassed an immense fortune, became one of the leading collectors and connoisseurs of paintings of his day. At his death in 1875, he bequeathed his collection to the nation and left the modern pictures to be sold. These included the famous *Duchess of Devonshire* by Gainsborough, which fetched 10,000 guineas under the hammer; Ellis had bought it for £46 in 1841. It was later stolen and discovered in America twenty-five years later where it was sold to Pierpont Morgan for £30,000.

Ellis had sold Ponsbourne to James W. Carlile just before his death. James Carlile came of a Scottish Presbyterian family and had made money in the Yorkshire woollen industry. He delighted in improving the estate when occasion arose and it was not long before he demolished the second mansion and erected the present house on the old foundations. In 1879 Ponsbourne was offered for sale by auction, but the offer was eventually withdrawn. The prospectus for the sale shows an estate of 549 acres of which 400 acres were pasture and only 84 acres arable, the principal farming being dairy.

It appears that James Carlile decided to stay on at Ponsbourne. In 1892 his first wife, Mary, died and on remarrying he decided to build a dower house on the south of the estate. This large red brick house, finished in 1897, is now known as Ponsbourne Manor. In 1906 the estate was sold to James' nephew, Sir Hildred Carlile, and James retired to the dower house where he died in 1909.

James Carlile's thirty years at Newgate Street really mark the beginning of a new, but short, era in the village. He was a benefactor both of the village and the church and his work was continued by his famous nephew. Sir Hildred Carlile, while resident at Ponsbourne, was Member of Parliament for Mid-Herts, and held numerous posts under the Governments of his day. He used his influence for the benefit of the district and county at large. As a brother of Prebendary Carlile, he was a keen supporter of the Church Army. Sir Hildred finally left Ponsbourne

Photo Henry Gray

Fig. 5. Ponsbourne House in the early 19th century
From a drawing in the Oldfleld collection, Hertford County Record Office.

Photo Kenneth Hutton

Fig. 6. Ponsbourne House as it is today

in 1932 and it was not long before the mansion was leased to the Roman Catholic Church as a convent school known as St. Dominic's Priory.

Ponsbourne Manor was occupied by the Misses Buxton after J. W. Carlile's time. They were followed by Mr. Hubert Pilkington and then by Mr. Menzies Sharpe, who founded the laboratory which is there now.

Between the wars much of the land was laid down as a golf course, but war meant cultivation for cereals and the extensive estates are now divided between the two farms of Howe Wood and Ponsbourne Park, both managed by members of the Sexton family. These farms are the successors of the three founded by Ewer in the seventeenth century.

Tolmers

Tolmers Manor, like Ponsbourne, originated in assarts. Its name commemorates the family, who probably made the first clearings in the wood. In 1251 a new assart belonged to Walter de Tolymer; it comprised thirty acres and was worth 10s. In 1277 Walter de Tolymer held land of the Bishop of Ely as a tenant-in-chief, and could pasture his cattle in the Great Wood. In 1308 John, William Tolymer's son, sold the land, which he had acquired from his brother William, to John the hayward of Hatfield manor. In 1327 the hayward conveyed the thirty acres to Roger de Luda and they were absorbed into Roger's Manor at Hornbeamgate, which lay to the north of Tylers Causeway. Tolmers was not separated from that manor until about 1406 when it was conveyed to Robert Chevall. The Chevall family had previously held two hides of land at Cromerhyde and they made a complete break by selling out this land and transferring their assets to Newgate Street, at that time a new, comparatively unknown part of Hatfield Manor. This step must have been made with many misgivings.

Besides the thirty acres from the Tolymer family, Chevall acquired a further thirty acres which, before the de Louths' ownership, was held by one Brice. Fifty-five more acres were included in Chevall's holding in Newgate Street; the whole a hundred and five acres yielded a rent of £1 3s. 11d.; this was a small estate, but formed a firm nucleus for the future Tolmers.

There is no record of the Chevalls' residence at Tolmers from 1406 to 1484, when Edmund Chyvall was paying suit of court at Hatfield. This indicates that Tolmers held the status of a sub-manor; it is probable that this had been the situation since 1406. As yet the manor was not described as Tolmers, and the first record of this is not until 1516. Early in the fifteenth century the first sizeable residence must have been built, probably of wattle and daub and on the site of the original dwelling of the Tolymers. It is probable that the Chevalls were influential in the district, the more so because of the absence of the Fortescues, who were active in the national government and wars of the period.

From its foundation the history of Tolmers is difficult to trace and especially so in the sixteenth century. Following a mention of Chyvall in 1484, the next reference is in 1516 when William Tattorn, who it appears held the freehold, enfeoffed the manor of Newgate Street alias Tolmers, consisting of 230 acres, to Sir William Say and his heir, Henry, Earl of Essex for their lives. No doubt, in the interim the Chyvalls had sold out to Tattorn, but all evidence seems to have disappeared.

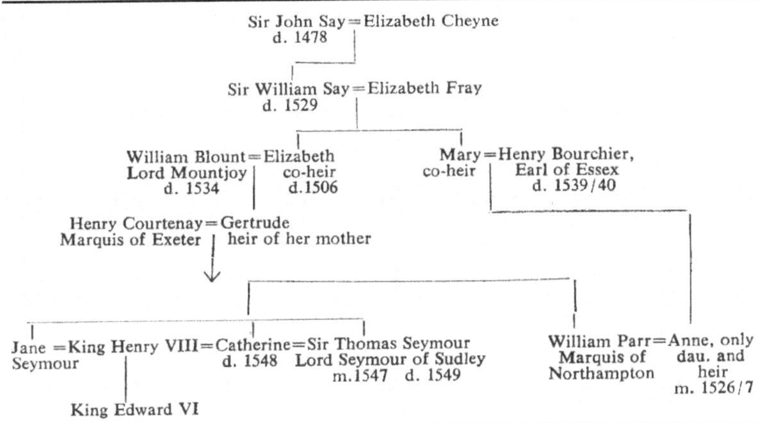

Fig. 7. Say family.

Sir William Say was the owner of the Manor of Bedwell Louths, which his father, Sir John, had established by amalgamating the Manors of Bedwell, Little Berkhamsted, Hornbeamgate and Blountes in 1466. Thus Tolmers was again linked with Hornbeamgate after a hundred years of separation. But this link did not last; Sir William died in 1529; Bedwell passed to his grand-daughter and Tolmers to his son-in-law the Earl of Essex. On the latter's death, in 1540, Tolmers descended to his daughter Anne, wife of William Parr, Marquis of Northampton. So it must be assumed that Essex had acquired the freehold title from Tattorn at some time during the tenancy.

From 1549 to 1588 the history of Tolmers touches on national history. Holders of the manor played leading parts in the politics and the government of the period. William Parr set the pattern by his activities during the minority of Edward VI. He was the brother of Catherine, last wife of Henry VIII and later wife of Sir Thomas Seymour of neighbouring Ponsbourne; Parr obtained the Earldom of Essex in 1543. He exercised great influence during Edward VI's reign and signed the letters which settled the crown on Lady Jane Grey. For this act, he was attainted in 1553 and Tolmers, along with all his other lands, was seized by the Crown. He had previously divorced Anne, his wife, but in 1555, Mary I regranted Tolmers in Anne's favour to be held in trust until her death.

On Anne's death in 1566, Tolmers reverted to the Crown and Elizabeth I exchanged it with her favourite Robert, Earl of Leicester, for land in Yorkshire. Leicester sold the reversion to Peter Osborne, of London, in July of the same year. Here, at Tolmers, is the first instance of a London merchant purchasing property in the neighbourhood. A London innkeeper had been tenant of Gacelyns in 1336; London merchants were buying Hertfordshire property from the early fourteenth century at least. By the sixteenth century they were founding many new County families. The purchase of properties became so competitive by the seventeenth century that Thomas Fuller complained: "that they who buy a house in Hertfordshire pay two years' purchase for the air"! But Osborne did not hold Tolmers for long; in January 1567 the reversion was sold to John Rumbold, yeoman. These quick sales were only of the reversion; Leicester continued to use Hill House, as it was then known. In 1587 he entertained Lady Arabella Stuart, niece to Mary, Queen of Scots; she was virtually kept as a prisoner, although Elizabeth I treated her as Princess Royal. Hill House was probably improved both internally and externally during the period of Leicester's interest in the manor. Some of the brickwork today appears to date from this period. The parkland may also have been laid out then.

Leicester died without heirs in 1588. Rumbold, while waiting for the reversion to fall in, bought a farm and 222 acres from William Clopton in 1572. In 1576 Audrey, daughter of John Rumbold, married Henry Goodere of Warwick and in the same year, Goodere was selling property in Whetstone for £1,850 with which to purchase "Tollemers". Rumbold died in 1580, but his widow continued to have an interest in the manor until 1606. It was not until 1608 that Sir Henry Goodere obtained a grant of the freehold title, which had reverted to the Crown on Leicester's death in 1588. Tolmers had been assessed at 12s. 2½d. in 1554; the assessment had risen to 16s. by 1597.

In his will, John Rumbold discharged all the debts of Goodere, which included money owed to Fulk Onslow. This gives a pointer to Goodere's spendthrift character. He was a typical Stuart courtier, perpetually in debt, and with a view to bettering his fortunes, he wrote many odes to people in high places. His literary talents seem to have procured him a knighthood and in 1608 Letters Patent from the Crown granting him the freehold of Tolmers. In 1626 he petitioned for a court post, asking for "only meat, drink and lodging, with some dignity, in that place (the court) where he had spent most of his time and estate".

In 1629 Francis Goodere succeeded to his father's estates and debts; he seems to have had the same spendthrift character. His fortunes went from bad to worse and his ingenuity in extracting himself from the mire led him to many sordid practices. His marriage to Catherine Onslow, of a wealthy Hatfield family, helped to stem the tide, but in 1630 Francis was in the courts for violently assaulting Jeremiah Barnes, which may have been due to financial differences. In 1633, he agreed to use his influence to get his kinswoman Jane Fountayne to marry John

Marston and for his pains £200 would be lent to him for twelve months without interest. He did persuade the lady and they left Newgate Street on horseback for St. Albans, where the marriage was to take place. But the pleasure was soon marred for on arriving at Colney the lady's horse stumbled, throwing her to the ground and killing her instantly. Needless to say, Goodere did not get his loan. He was again in court in 1635 for not paying one year's wages of £4 to his servant Andrew Moore.

By 1639 Goodere was forced to mortgage his estate to Robert Shiers, barrister of London. In 1649 Goodere sold the estate to Shiers for £2,750, repaying his mortgage. But Goodere's troubles were not over. In 1650 he was fined £40 for trespassing and trying to force a tenant William Brice to pay rent.

From 1649 until 1668 the documents of the manor although very abundant are very conflicting. But at various times Henry Goodere, Robert Shiers, William Dawgs and James Baron are reputed to be the owners. The manor probably benefitted from William Dawgs' possession. He was a co-deputy receiver of the Duchy of Lancaster and a large land-owner in the County. He proceeded to add considerable lands to the manor, a common practice among puritans during the Commonwealth. In 1668, Robert Shiers died possessed of Tolmers and was succeeded by his son Sir George Shiers. It is very probable that Shiers held the absolute freehold title throughout the period 1649-68 and that the people mentioned above only held reversionary leases which reverted to Shiers after 1662. At Sir George Shiers' death in 1690 all of his estates in Hatfield, Digswell and Welwyn were placed in the hands of trustees for the benefit of the poor of the parishes of Bookham and Fetcham in Surrey. In 1714 Hugh Shortridge, one of the trustees under Shiers' will, conveyed Tolmers to another trustee. In 1802 Sir William Geary, as trustee, sold Tolmers by auction for £2,655.

Tolmers or Hill House seems to have been a larger building than Ponsbourne after the improvements probably made by Leicester. This was definitely the case in 1663. The Hearth Tax Survey shows that Tolmers had fourteen hearths to Ponsbourne's eleven, implying that Tolmers had more rooms and probably a greater floor space. Although Tolmers may have been the larger building it was also the smaller manor. During the sixteenth century the area is constant at 230 acres. In 1610, when Hatfield Great Wood was converted into farmland, Sir Henry Goodere was granted an additional seventy acres on losing his common rights in the wood, and the area of Tolmers has stayed constant from then: in 1802 it is described as 320 acres, in 1838 as 318 acres.

During the Trusteeship, five persons leased and farmed the land and lived in the house in succession. They were James Parnell, Thomas Burgess, Christopher Buckle, Philip Ansell and Matthew Arbon. It is interesting to note that the manor was sold in 1662 for £2,600 and in 1802 for £2,655. It is possible that Garnet Terry purchased Tolmers in 1802 as an investment for there is no evidence that he or his successor,

Margaret Mouseley, lived there. Their tenant from 1803 to 1836 was Robert Taylor; he was a Justice of the Peace and was granted a certificate for killing game.

In 1827 Tolmers was purchased by Charles Dimsdale; it was sold to Samuel Mills in 1834. He was succeeded by his eldest son Thomas Mills, M.P., in 1847 and, on the latter's death, by a younger son John Remington Mills. Each of these owners of Tolmers was a partner in the London banking firm of Glyn, Mills and Company and they each endeavoured to enrich the estate and district. The lodge and sundry cottages were built during this period and the hamlet benefitted by the building of its church in 1847 by Thomas Mills. John Remington Mills died in 1879 and the freehold passed to his daughters. By 1868 Sir Thomas Bazley, M.P., was living in Tolmers, probably under a lease, and it was at his instigation that the house was rebuilt to its present appearance.

Following Sir Thomas, five tenants lived at Tolmers before it was eventually converted into a private girls' school between the wars. By 1937 Tolmers was closed as a school and it remained vacant until it was taken over as a hospital in 1940; it was later purchased by the County Council as a hospital for old people. At present the building houses about eighty persons, both patients and staff, and provides occupation for some villagers (Fig. 8).

Fig. 8. Tolmers *Photo* Henry Gray

During the seventeenth and eighteenth centuries the farm lands on the Tolmers estate were known as Rucks farm, after the first tenant. This name appears to have fallen into disuse and today the farm is known as Tolmers Park farm; it is worked by Mr. Brooks of Home Farm.

The Farms and the Village

The principal occupation of the district has always been farming and until this century the population has been exclusively devoted to the land. The terrain of the district is not ideal for working, being predominantly heavy blue clay, either on the surface or underneath a pebbly top-soil. In a series of consistently bad summers cereal farming operations get completely bogged down; machinery sticks in the mud. During a dry summer, machinery will not touch the iron-hard surface. It is possible that these conditions may account for the rapid turnover of farmers in the district. Of recent years it is known that two farmers, both experts at their job, have found that farming on the high ground on the west side of the parish has been uneconomic.

Local farms have gone through three phases. At first small holdings were created out of the forest in assarts, as we have seen. Then most of the holdings were absorbed into two sub-manors; the subordinate farms of the two estates still remain. In 1610 the enclosure of Hatfield Great Wood produced the biggest social and economic upheaval in Newgate Street history; it led to the creation of new farms.

Until 1610 all the land to the west of the Northaw-Little Berkhamsted Road was part of Hatfield Great Wood. It was heavily afforested and stocked with deer, and various tenants of Hatfield Manor had certain common rights in the wood. In 1610 the Earl of Salisbury decided to enclose much of the Great Wood and the commoners were compensated by grants of land. Many Newgate Street inhabitants were affected by this reorganization and about 213 acres were allotted to them. The Earl formed the eastern part of the enclosed area into the New Park of 560 acres, stocking it with deer and conies; he leased it to a keeper, Sir Antonie Forrest. As a park, New Park was not a success and between 1610 and 1692 at least seven persons held the lease. In 1692 it is first described as a farm, NEW PARK FARM; the Park had been abandoned. As a farm it prospered; only three leaseholders held the land before 1760; but the last century has been a return to rapid change in tenancies (Fig. 1, p. 4).

Until the enclosure of New Park the main road to Hatfield from Cheshunt had always been along the route of the old Roman Road, i.e. along New Park Road joining the present road at Woodfield. With the enclosure a lodge gate was erected in 1620, where the road entered the New Park.

It is possible that New Park was formed into a farm in 1626, for in that year COLDHARBOUR FARM of about 226 acres was cut out of the New Park. Part of its land included Friday Field and the derelict moated site of the Hornbeamgate manor-house. The exposed situation would probably account for the name of the farm. The nature of the soil may account for some of its gruesome field names—Kill Devil, Little Ease, Hell Ley, Long Pain and Deadmans Small Gains. Like New Park,

Coldharbour has had many tenants, few of whom have stayed for long periods.

The land granted by Salisbury to the holders of Tolmers and Ponsbourne in exchange for their common rights in the Great Wood consisted of 150 acres, all the land between the New Park and the Little Berkhamsted Road, and was known as the Falls. The southern portion of this land, 75 acres, is first recorded as a farm in 1631 and it was held of Ponsbourne. In 1658 the farm was sold separately from the Manor, to Mathew Turner for £780 and became PONSFALL FARM. In 1695, Ponsfall was granted by Gift to Christs Hospital and remained in their hands until 1935, when it was sold by auction to the tenant B. Robinson Sawyer, whose son still holds the land. Many tenants have farmed the land and during this century the farm was used as a research station.

HOME FARM or TOLMERS FARM, like Ponsfall, was also created from land granted by Lord Salisbury after 1610, this time to the owners of Tolmers. At the present time, Archibald Brooks, the tenant at Home Farm, also farms all the agricultural land on the Tolmers Manor estate.

Photo Barbara Hutton

Fig. 9. The Blacksmith's forge at Newgate Street

Where there is farming there is a *blacksmith* and there is no doubt that one had his forge in Newgate Street from early days. By 1870 there were two in the hamlet, a farrier at the Coach and Horses and a smith adjacent to the Crown. Today, the farrier Walter Bright still plies his trade, especially on Saturday mornings, shoeing horses from riding schools and hunts from an area of up to 10 miles radius. During the past forty years, he has also run a bus service to neighbouring towns, a vocation terminated by an accident. The neighbouring petrol station is in the hands of Mr. L. B. Smith, who also runs a car-hire service.

The late fourteenth century saw the disappearance of the many small holdings and the growth of Newgate Street hamlet into a community supplying labour for the neighbouring sub-manors. This probably brought a sense of stability and permanence to the inhabitants, which is reflected in the reference to a villager made in 1482 in the Hatfield Court Rolls—Richard Salver was fined for brewing ale. In 1484, John Hoo committed the same offence. He was accused of brewing and selling. Evidently local ale-houses were beginning to develop and the community was making attempts to regulate abuses. In 1609 Roger Nelson of Newgate Street was in trouble for keeping an unlicensed alehouse. There is another long gap in the evidence until the eighteenth century, but Newgate Street undoubtedly had ale to drink and the social life which went with drinking.

The first record of the COACH AND HORSES (front cover) is of 1756 and a billeting return made for the War Office shows that Warrand Tipping was the licensee; the building had one spare bed and stabling for two horses. It is very probable that the present building dates from this period. By 1817 Daniel Byford had the licence; his descendants are still living in the district. From 1855 to 1891 the licence frequently changed hands, but in 1891 William Petty took over and his descendants have been there ever since. The house has always been the principal pub of the village but since the advent of the motor car it has also become a fashionable inn for summer evening trippers.

The CROWN cannot be dated earlier than 1811 and the licence, which was held until 1938, was a cottage licence only. In 1851 the Publican was also the local coal merchant. In 1938 the old building, an inn with house attached, was demolished and replaced by the present building. Of its many inmates, probably Abraham Wackett was the most noted. He held the Crown in the 1860's and later took to farming at Tylers Causeway. His ancestors had lived for centuries in the district and many of his descendants can still be found in the County. Opposite the Crown Inn stood the village pump; one villager at least remembers the village children being regularly washed here.

Until 1955 a beerhouse, the ROSE AND CROWN, served the Tylers Causeway community. The first record of this house is in 1851, and the Payne family held the licence for many years during the first half of this century. Mrs. Cross, the last licensee, will long be remembered in the village for her stentorian voice. Following its closure as a public house the Rose and Crown was, for a short time, a cafe and is now a private residence.

THE CHURCH was late in coming to Newgate Street, and until that event the villagers had to make the long trek to Hatfield or Little Berkhamsted for their spiritual guidance. There is a record of a Primitive Methodist chapel in 1829, and this still existed in 1851, after the present church was built, in 1847, by Thomas Mills of Tolmers. The land had been granted by Wynn Ellis out of the Ponsbourne Estate, hence the church's dedication to St. Mary's Ponsbourne. The church became an outpost chapel of Hatfield Parish and a perpetual curate took up residence at the Vicarage.

In 1912, through the instigation of Sir Hildred Carlile, Newgate Street was segregated from Hatfield Parish to form a separate ecclesiastical parish. In 1959 the third important event happened to the church, when it was decided to convert the Vicarage into a college for pre-ordination candidates of the Church of England and the Rev. Norman Hillyer was appointed warden and vicar of the parish. This event promises to have a marked effect on the village in the future.

THE SCHOOL was built at the same time as the church, also by Mills, as a church school for boys and girls. At the latter end of the last century the average attendance was thirty pupils between six and thirteen years of age. Today the County Council controls the school and average attendance is still thirty pupils but between five and eleven.

The first reference to a *village store* is made in 1851 when Joseph Turner, the local carpenter, retailed from his cottage opposite the Crown: in 1868 George Bennett was retailing in the same way. Law and order came to the village, in the shape of the village constable, very early in its history. In 1542, a worthy named Catemoye was appointed constable by the Ponsbourne Manor Court. Various references are made to other constables at different times—Thomas Hossman in 1663, William Barrelegs in 1685, George Cook in 1879. Today the local policeman serves both Newgate Street and Little Berkhamsted.

It is of interest that on 16th April, 1879 (Easter Day) a cricket match was played in Newgate Street. "The cricketers would have played upon the village green, but for the simple fact that what is left of the green is but about a dozen paces in length. Like a good many places, Newgate Street lost its green years ago." The commencement of the match had been in doubt, because snow had fallen heavily on the previous day!

As long as each parish was responsible for the maintenance of its own highways, their upkeep was always a bone of contention. There are many recorded cases, in the Quarter Sessions Records during the seventeenth century, of the villagers not doing their share of work in the maintenance of roads in Hatfield Manor. Finally in 1667 a commissioned group of independent observers decided that the villagers were duty bound to maintain five miles of the *Great North Road*. In 1825 Robert Taylor reported that the road at the bottom of Darnicle Hill "is ruinous, deep broken and in great decay", but the people of Cheshunt were found responsible for this. About 1826 the bridge known as Postern Gate, over Grimes Brook, was erected and, although it was the responsibility of the County, from 1869 to 1886 this bridge was continually in need of repair.

The railway line, which, it was decided in 1895, to build from Wood Green to Stevenage, reached Cuffley in 1910 and negotiations were opened to take the track across Ponsbourne Park, building a Halt at the bottom of Darnicle Hill to serve Newgate Street. Both of these schemes were strongly objected to by Sir Hildred Carlile. Consequently Ponsbourne Tunnel was constructed under the Park and the village went without a station. The tunnel was built during the early part of the 1914-1918 War, work being carried on day and night. Although the line was used from 1917, it was not officially opened to passenger traffic until 1924.

Life in Newgate Street altered very little until the last century. The population had probably been about sixty for four centuries. In the 1840's, when Wynn Ellis and the Mills family were the local squires, the village took on a new lease of life. By 1868 the population had risen to about 150 people and the hamlet was becoming more of a village; at the same time its dependence on neighbouring communities was increaseing.

Fifty years later, the railway reached the district and the labour to build it was housed in the village and nearby. More houses were built to accommodate them, which ultimately meant a small increase in the population. The rejection of the proposal for a halt on the line has meant that suburbia has not reached this rural part of Hertfordshire and there has never been any housing development for the city worker as at neighbouring Cuffley. Since the 1939-1945 War this contrast has been further emphasised by the inclusion of Newgate Street in the Metropolitan Green Belt area. Excluding the inmates of Tolmers and Ponsbourne, the population at present is about 650 people, an increase which mainly came about between the wars. Since the last war, only a small amount of property has been erected.

Until the turn of the century, agriculture or domestic work at the big houses had been the only occupations of the villagers. But during this century two industries have been introduced—the St. James Tile Company producing terrazzo tiles, and the laboratory which has been set up in Ponsbourne Manor to produce pharmaceutical tablets. Both draw on local people for their labour. But the de Havilland Aircraft Factory at Hatfield is the biggest attraction for labour; it has taken many people from the land. It has taken families away from Newgate Street, but there are still many people who travel from the village into Hatfield every day.

A certain proportion of the population are still working on the farms, but there is another section of the community who travel to the Lea Valley, working in the nurseries. This includes the displaced persons living in the camp in New Park Road, the lease of which is held by the Lea Valley Growers' Association. There are also some villagers employed in Tolmers Hospital. Due primarily to the inducement of better jobs outside the village, the population appears to be constantly mobile and it is noticeable that very few families can trace their ancestry back in the village more than a century. This is not merely a modern trend and it implies that there is little in the district to hold people. The communal spirit found in many country villages is not so predominant in Newgate

Street; there has been a decline in this respect since the Carliles' departure from Ponsbourne.

This history would not be complete without some mention of the 1939-45 war years in Newgate Street. On 25th September, 1940, a land mine dropped in New Park Road, demolishing many houses, but fortunately causing only minor casualties. The upheaval caused much concern at the time but the scars have now healed and new cottages stand on the sites of the old. About this time a camp was erected to house Italian and, later, German Prisoners of War, who used to work on the local farms. Much of the surrounding landscape was marred by military defence works, part of the outer defences of London, and some of them are only now being removed.

Although Newgate Street has developed into a small distinct community, it is still very dependent upon its parent Hatfield and other neighbouring towns. Besides supplying work, Hatfield still administers our Local Government. But as public transport to the town from the village is non-existent, Newgate Street is compelled to look to Hertford for sustenance and it is to the County Town that the villagers go for their shopping excursions.

GERALD MILLINGTON

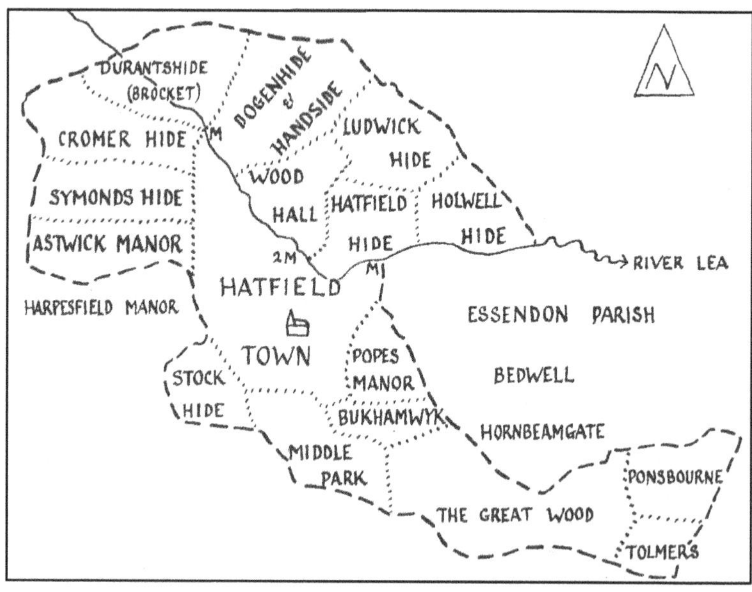

Fig. 10. The manors of Ponsbourne and Tolmers (Newgate Street) showing their position in Hatfield Parish in the middle ages. Scale ½"= 1 mile.

INDEX

Note: Page numbers in *italics* indicate illustrations;

www.ingramcontent.com/pod-product-compliance
Ingram Content Group UK Ltd.
Pitfield, Milton Keynes, MK11 3LW, UK
UKHW020227250726
13967UKWH00001B/225